T0082137

Runners run on
tracks at athletic events.

Sprints are very short.

They are 100m or 200m.

The runners crouch on the starting blocks, and sprint off as soon as the starting gun is heard.

Some runs are long,
as long as 10,000m.

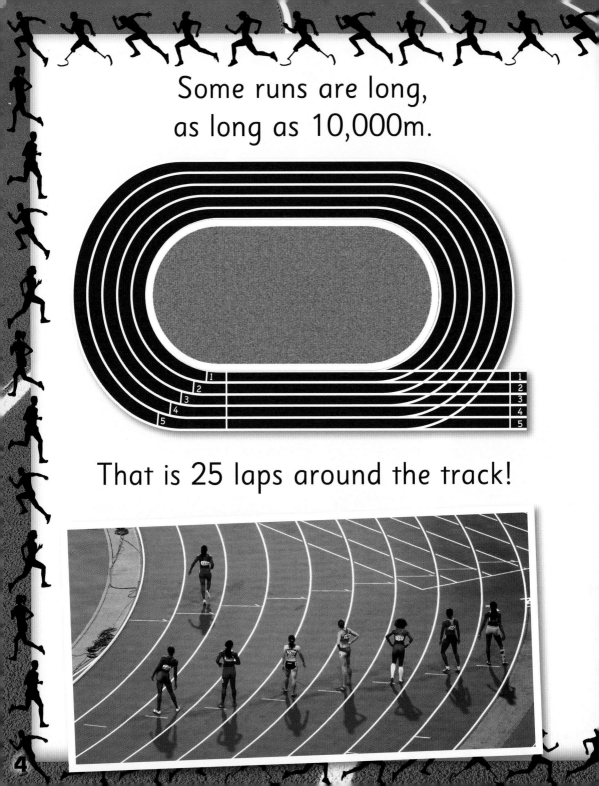

That is 25 laps around the track!

relay
/reelai/

In relays, a baton is handed from runner to runner.

baton

They must have the baton to run, and they must not drop it.

A marathon is a very long run.

Marathons are often run on roads.
The best competitors can run
them in about 2 hours!

racing wheelchair
/**rai**sing **wee**lcheɛr/

There are wheelchair marathons too.

Some marathons have
hundreds of runners in them.

Some are "fun runners" and
run in funny outfits to raise
funds for charity.

santa fun run

For fun runners, 4 hours is good
– but some just aim to finish!

In cross country running, you run along outdoor trails. It can be very muddy!

Cross country tends not to be very long, but you run across different tracks: flat, hilly, muddy, sandy...

Canicross is cross country running with your dog!

The dogs have harnesses that attach to the runner.